THE JAPANESE IN AMERICA

THE JAPANESE
IN AMERICA

Noel L. Leathers

Lerner Publications Company · Minneapolis

Front cover: Members of the large Kumagai clan came from all over the United States to attend a family reunion in Denver. Pictured here (left to right) are Craig, Toshiko, and Jennifer Takaoka of Palatine, Illinois.

Page 2: A small Japanese-American boy from San Francisco had his identity tag checked by federal authorities in April 1942–just before he and his family were relocated by bus to the Tanforan Assembly Center in California.

1991 REVISED EDITION

The Library of Congress cataloged the original printing of this title as follows:

Leathers, Noel L.
  The Japanese in America [by] Noel L. Leathers.
Minneapolis, Lerner Publications Co. [1967]

  70 p. illus., ports. 24 cm. (The In America series)

  This volume examines the life of Japanese immigrants in America, their wartime contributions, their life in relocation centers, the discrimination they have met and their numerous contributions to the development of America despite this injustice. Also discusses the life of the Japanese in Hawaii.
  1. Japanese in the U. S. I. Title
E184.J3L4   j301.453   67-15684

ISBN: 0-8225-0241-0 [Library]
ISBN: 0-8225-1042-1 [Paper]

Manufactured in the United States of America

8 9 10 11 12 13 14 15 16 17 00 99 98 97 96 95 94 93 92 91

CONTENTS

1 **JAPANESE IMMIGRATION TO AMERICA**   6
   Generation after Generation   *6*
   Japan and the West   *8*
   Reasons for Emigration   *11*

2 **AN AMERICAN WAY OF LIFE**   14
   Finding a Place   *14*
   Farming   *15*
   Fishing   *17*
   Commerce   *18*
   Building Communities   *19*
   Picture Brides   *22*

3 **PREJUDICE AND WAR**   24
   A Longstanding Problem   *24*
   The San Francisco School Controversy   *25*
   The Gentlemen's Agreement and Land Laws   *28*
   The Coming of War   *29*
   Evacuation   *33*
   Relocation Centers   *35*
   A Different War   *38*
   Civilian Contributions   *43*
   The End of Internment   *43*
   After the War   *44*
   New Contact with Japan   *46*

4 **CONTRIBUTIONS TO AMERICAN LIFE**   48
   Government and Public Affairs   *48*
   Business   *51*
   Science, Education, and Scholarship   *52*
   Architecture, Art, and Literature   *53*
   Music   *56*
   Sports and Entertainment   *58*

INDEX   61
ACKNOWLEDGMENTS   63

1
JAPANESE IMMIGRATION TO AMERICA

Mariko Savitt (left) and her sister Leilani, who are of partial Japanese ancestry, visit their grandmother, Kikue Ogasawara, who lives in Seattle, Washington.

Generation after Generation

Japan lies directly across the Pacific Ocean from the United States. The southernmost islands of Japan are about as far south as the Florida Keys, and the northernmost point in Japan is about as far north as Portland, Oregon. Through most of this north-south range, winds usually blow from Japan toward the United States. Also at these latitudes, several strong currents—streams of ocean water—flow east from Japan across the Pacific. Sea traders and fishing fleets from many nations learned to exploit these winds and currents to travel from East Asia toward North America. Japanese sea-farers were among them.

The first Japanese to come to the United States were accidental visitors—shipwreck survivors who were rescued by U.S. vessels. The first recorded arrival of a Japanese in the United States was in 1843, when a ship-wrecked sailor named Manjiro Nakahama was rescued and brought to port in Massachusetts. Several such incidents occurred in the 1840s and 1850s, but they involved only a few sailors. Even fewer of these Japanese actually stayed on to live permanently in the United States. The number of

Japanese immigrants grew only very slowly, and by 1880 fewer than 150 lived in the U.S.

This number stayed so low partly because, through much of the 19th century, it was illegal for most Japanese to emigrate from their home country. In 1885, however, the Japanese government eased its restrictions on emigration. The number of Japanese in the United States and Hawaii (which was not yet part of the United States) then increased rapidly. Each year during the 1890s, on average, the number of Japanese entering the United States increased by about 1,000 over the

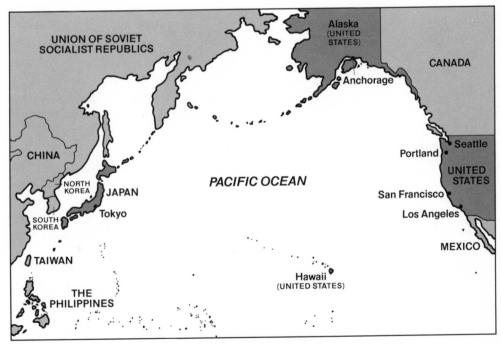

Japan lies directly across the Pacific Ocean from the United States.

number who had entered during the previous year. In 1900, more than 12,000 Japanese entered the U.S.

From 1900 to 1907, Japanese who had previously gone to Hawaii were relatively free to come to the United States mainland if they pleased. Beginning in 1908, however, an agreement between the U.S. and Japanese governments banned any new influx of Japanese laborers from Hawaii. In 1924, immigration of Japanese was virtually halted when a harsh new immigration law was passed by the U.S. Congress to prohibit the entry of Asians. Not until the late 1940s, after World War II, did any significant immigration of Japanese to America resume.

According to the U.S. Immigration and Naturalization Service, only 450,359 Japanese immigrated to the United States between 1820 and 1988. This number is quite small, even in relation to the numbers of immigrants from other Asian nations. Japanese immigrants to the United States constitute less than 10 percent of the total of Asian immigrants between 1820 and 1988.

In the 1980 U.S. census, 791,275 Americans claimed to have at least one Japanese ancestor. About 84 percent of these persons—666,856 of them—claimed only Japanese ancestry, without any other ethnic background mixed in.

Japanese immigrants to the United States—as is traditional among the people of Japan—nurture a strong awareness of their ancestry. Japanese Americans even classify themselves into specific groups depending on how many generations have passed since a person's family immigrated to the United States.

The Japanese word *Issei* (pronounced ee-SAY) is used for any person who was born in Japan but later moved to another country—a first-generation immigrant. A *Nisei* (pronounced nee-SAY) is an immigrant's son or daughter who was born outside Japan. The third generation, the *Sansei* (sahn-SAY), are the daughters and sons of the Nisei. The *Yonsei* (yahn-SAY) are the fourth generation, the children of the Sansei.

Japan and the West

Through most of history, Japan's leaders chose to keep their island empire isolated from the rest of the world. The government prevented foreigners from visiting Japan and the Japanese people from leaving.

This isolation ended, however, after the arrival of an American naval officer, Commodore Matthew C. Perry. Eager to to establish a trading relationship with the Japanese and to protect American sailors in the North Pacific, Perry led a group of U.S. warships into Edo Bay (now known as Tokyo Bay) in 1853. Perry demanded that the Japanese government establish commercial and diplomatic ties with the United States. Then he sailed away,

北亞墨利加人物
ペルリ像

A Japanese artist portrayed Commodore Matthew C. Perry, an American naval commander, like this. In 1853, Perry first made contact with the Japanese—a meeting that would eventually bring Japan into the mainstream of world trade.

promising to return in the following spring to hear the answer to his proposal. Perry returned—accompanied by even more warships—and the answer was yes. In 1854, the United States became the first Western nation to conclude a treaty—the Treaty of Kanagawa—establishing diplomatic relations with the Japanese. This was followed four years later by a major trade agreement, the Edo Treaty.

Japanese society at this time was in flux. The government—headed by a leader known as the shogun—was overthrown in 1867 by a group of militants. In the following year, the rebel leaders installed a 15-year-old boy, whose name was Mutsuhito, as emperor. This young sovereign then chose for himself a new title, Meiji. The time during which he was emperor (1868-1912) is therefore called the Meiji period. During the Meiji period, the Japanese government greatly increased the nation's contacts with the outside world.

To modernize Japan, the government sent intelligent young Japanese abroad to study Western technology and business practices. They went to many nations, including the United States, Great Britain, Prussia, France, and Russia. From each of these countries, the Japanese adopted what they thought would be most useful to them—the sewage and sanitation systems of Philadelphia, Pennsylvania; the medical practices and the constitution of Prussia; the street layouts and traffic

To impress Japanese officials, American troops paraded just outside a temple in Shimoda, Japan, on June 8, 1854.

patterns of Great Britain; the military organization of France.

Modernization brought both benefits and problems to Japan. Japan's many new factories needed large amounts of raw materials and fuel. Japan's own supplies of iron ore and energy resources, for example, were nowhere near enough to satisfy this demand. To get the raw materials they needed, the Japanese government decided to expand their control over nearby territory—most of which was under Russian or Chinese rule. Japan won several wars and skirmishes with China and Russia, and the Japanese eventually gained control over many nearby islands, the Korean Peninsula, and several coastal parts of eastern China. By the end of the Russo-Japanese War (1904-1905), the formerly isolated Japanese had become major rivals of other Asian nations and of the West.

Reasons for Emigration

While Japan was building its empire by conquering nearby territory, the Japanese also saw nonmilitary opportunities overseas. Japanese businesspersons, government officials, and sailors noticed, for example, that many fast-growing nations, especially in the Americas, were short of laborers for their farms and factories. The pay for such overseas work was usually much higher than pay for comparable work in Japan. As early as the late 1860s, Japanese contract laborers were taking jobs on the plantations of Hawaii or other islands in the Pacific.

These workers who went overseas were often called "emigrants," but this term is somewhat misleading. Emigrants are usually thought of as people who leave their homeland in order to reside permanently in another country. Many of the workers who left Japan, however, did not want to immigrate—to become permanent residents of the countries where they worked. They wanted only to work overseas for a while, make their money, and return to Japan.

The Japanese government considered itself responsible for these workers even after they had gone overseas. In fact, according to Japanese law, anyone with a Japanese father was still a Japanese subject, regardless of where he or she happened to reside. Almost as soon as laborers started to take jobs outside Japan, mistreatment of these workers became a problem. The plantation owners in Hawaii, in particular, were accused of treating their Japanese workers like slaves. The Japanese government responded in 1868 by halting the emigration of laborers to Hawaii.

In 1885, however, the Japanese government dramatically changed its policy. Hawaii at that time, despite the many American businesses and plantations operating there, was not part of the United States. (Hawaii was an independent kingdom until 1893, was annexed by the U.S. in 1898, and set up a territorial government under U.S. law in 1900.) Hawaii's royal government, eager to import laborers for the Hawaiian sugar plantations, gave the Japanese government permission to inspect working conditions on the plantations. With greater power to prevent abuses to workers, the Japanese government not only agreed to let laborers go to Hawaii but also helped transport them there.

Some private companies—called emigration companies—also made a business of finding jobs for laborers and shipping these workers overseas. Such workers were called *contract laborers* because, at the time they left Japan, they had already signed an agreement (a contract) to work for a certain company. An emigration company charged each employer a fee for supplying workers. Sometimes the companies also collected fees from the workers or from their families.

By 1894, the Japanese government was transporting very few contract workers to Hawaii. Almost every laborer who went to Hawaii did so under the sponsorship of a private emigration company. Some of these companies, however, cheated the workers. For example, a Japanese contract worker might be delivered overseas only to discover that his salary was much lower than the emigration company had promised. To stop this cheating, the Japanese government imposed strict regulations on the emigration companies in 1896. Even after that time, however, the emigration companies prospered. The number of

workers they shipped to Hawaii—the prime destination for contract laborers —between 1896 and 1907 was probably between 70,000 and 100,000.

Many contract laborers were also sent to the West Coast of the United States—especially California, Oregon, Washington, and the Territory of Alaska—but not as openly as to Hawaii. Even though there was a lot of work for laborers (especially on the railroads, on farms, and in fish canneries), it was against U.S. law for a laborer to enter the United States from Japan with a job already lined up. The Japanese government, not wanting to anger U.S. officials, issued only a limited

Japanese laborers on a Hawaiian sugar plantation in the 1890s

number of passports for contract workers to go to the United States. Even if a Japanese contract laborer could get a passport, he or she still had to get past U.S. immigration officials after crossing the Pacific. Many laborers were refused entry to the U.S. because they failed to conceal their employment arrangements. Others managed to get through.

Contract laborers, however, were not the only Japanese traveling to the United States. Even when the laws of Japan banned the emigration of contract workers, other Japanese citizens were permitted to leave. Although U.S. law did not permit the immigration of contract laborers from Japan, other Japanese citizens could enter. A few enterprising Japanese set up their own businesses in the United States. Some Japanese trading companies and banks set up U.S. offices and sent Japanese to the United States to manage them.

Students were another relatively large group of Japanese in the United States. Some Japanese students— especially those with scholarships from the Japanese government— attended such prestigious U.S. colleges as Harvard, Cornell, and Princeton. Like most laborers, the majority of these privileged Japanese were not immigrants; they intended only to get an education and then return to their native country. Not every Japanese student in the U.S., however, was a scholarship holder. Some adventurous young Japanese— many of whom wanted a higher education but could not win admission to any Japanese university—came on their own to the U.S. to study. Although some came from wealthy families, many of these students had to take jobs in order to pay their way through school. A large number of these working students eventually decided to stay in the United States.

Other groups of Japanese who came to the United States were unhappy with life in Japan and were looking for a new place to settle. The social changes that took place in Japan at the start of the Meiji period displaced many of Japan's old rulers and nobles. Some of these people, having lost much of their wealth and their social position, were eager to make a new start somewhere else. Some active opponents of the new government found it healthier to leave for America than to stay in Japan. Other people saw no future for themselves in an increasingly industrial Japan except at a monotonous job in a dreary factory. Others were in danger of being drafted for military service and chose to leave rather than serve in the army or navy. For these and other reasons, many Japanese people decided to leave their homeland and not return.

2
AN AMERICAN WAY OF LIFE

Japanese-descended farm workers outside their California home, 1911

Finding a Place

The Japanese, like immigrants from other countries, were often disappointed by life in Hawaii or the United States. The great wealth and wonderful life they had expected were very different from what they actually found.

Immigrants who came under the authority of an emigration company were lined up as soon as they stepped off their ship. They were then marched off in military fashion to the company's barracks. From there they were assigned as laborers wherever the contractor needed them. Employers liked Japanese contract laborers because they would work for lower wages than other laborers would accept. Non-Japanese laborers, however, grew to resent the Japanese for getting so much of the available work and for helping to keep wages low. This resentment made life uncomfortable for the

Japanese in America and would later swell into a dangerous tide of racism.

Japanese students who needed to work their way through college became domestic servants or took other work that might leave them enough time to attend classes. Skilled Japanese went to live in the cities, where they pursued such professions as carpentry and accounting. By 1902, more than 350 Japanese Americans also worked as doctors, lawyers, dentists, and professors. Even the skilled workers and students found American life difficult. The English language presented a major obstacle. Widespread prejudice against Asians restricted the Japanese and made them feel not only unwelcome but also threatened.

Still, despite all the trials of life in Hawaii and the United States, the Japanese persevered and became quite successful in numerous fields.

Farming

Many of the newly arrived Japanese became farm workers. Most of the immigrants had come from small villages and rural areas in Japan where farming was the chief way of earning a living. Fast-growing farms in the western United States badly needed laborers, and the Japanese had a reputation as excellent farm workers.

The Japanese workers also benefited from the misfortunes of the Chinese. In 1882, the U.S. Congress passed a law called the Chinese Exclusion Act, which stopped immigration to the U.S. from China. Congress was responding to widespread complaints in the United States that Chinese labor would flood the market and leave no jobs for U.S. citizens. The act caused a labor shortage in the western United States, particularly in California. Those U.S. employers who were able to hire Japanese laborers found them to be excellent, low-cost replacements for the Chinese.

Many Japanese who arrived in Hawaii or the United States as almost penniless laborers became landholders within a very short time. After saving what they had earned as laborers, they might move one step up by becoming sharecroppers (persons who work a farm owned by someone else and who are allowed to keep some of what they grow). If they were successful as sharecroppers, they might decide to go one step further and lease a farm. Finally, once they had enough cash, they might buy a farm outright. Buying their own land was a major move toward prestige and independence. For Japanese men who wanted to stay in the United States and raise families, it was sometimes a necessity. The Japanese government would not permit women to emigrate from Japan to marry poor laborers, but Japanese women were allowed to emigrate to marry the owner of a successful farm.

By 1920, people of Japanese descent in California owned nearly 75,000 acres (30,375 hectares) and leased more than 383,000 acres (155,115 hectares). Even though this was a respectable amount of land, it made up only a small percentage of California's farmland. Moreover, the size of the average farm worked by Japanese immigrants was only 56 acres (22.7 hectares), while the average West Coast farm was much larger—320 acres (129.6 hectares). Most Japanese farms in America, however, were successful not because of their size but because of their productivity. By applying Japan's traditional techniques of intensive farming—ways of getting a high yield from a small parcel of land—the Japanese became major producers of many vegetables and fruits. In 1910, for example, just under three-quarters of California's strawberries were produced by the Japanese.

One example of the Japanese success at high-yield farming is the agricultural community of Vacaville, California. Vacaville, in the Vaca Valley southwest of Sacramento, had originally been settled by immigrants from Scandinavia. With an adverse climate and poor soil conditions, however, its farms were poor. Then, beginning in 1888, several Japanese farmers decided to move to Vacaville.

The Japanese families who settled in the Vacaville area were determined to make something out of this wasteland. They fertilized the soil several times each year. They planted fruit trees and sprayed them over and over

*A Japanese farm worker harvesting cabbages in Hawaii in the 1960s still had some things in common with his predecessors of the 1890s. His shoulder yoke, used to carry the harvest, was one; the traditional **tabis** (stocking shoes) on his feet were another.*

instead of the usual once per season. They developed irrigation channels and supplied this farmland with four or five times more water than it had ever been given before. Within five years, the Japanese Americans had transformed the area around Vacaville into one of the most profitable farming regions in California.

Fishing

While many Japanese were building reputations as excellent farmers, others were establishing themselves in the fishing industry. Japan's own fleets had long fished the Pacific, so many of the immigrants had considerable shipboard experience. Others

Japanese-American tuna fishermen from Hawaii having a shipboard lunch

found work processing or packing the catch. One of the centers of Japanese fishing activity was Terminal Island in Los Angeles Harbor.

In 1901, a dozen Japanese came to Terminal Island and began catching fish and gathering abalone (a sea animal plentiful off the California coast). The Japanese at Terminal Island built homes on stilts driven into the water along the shore. Their business grew rapidly. By 1910, there were three canneries operating on the island, and the population had reached 3,000. While the fleets were at sea, other Japanese worked in the canneries,

cleaning and packing fish for metropolitan Los Angeles. The fleets fished extensive areas of the Pacific Ocean from Central America to Hawaii. By the beginning of World War II, 60 percent of the population of Terminal Island was of Japanese ancestry.

Commerce

Trade, especially in the wholesale market for fruits and vegetables, became another major occupation for the Japanese Americans. Sometimes, non-Japanese wholesalers refused to

A Japanese-American market in Los Angeles continued the immigrant community's long involvement in marketing fresh fruits and vegetables.

Japanese workers in Hawaii often did their laundry at streams near their housing compounds.

buy vegetables and fruit from Japanese-American farmers, so Japanese Americans went into the wholesale business to provide an outlet for the produce of these boycotted farmers. In this way, Japanese Americans gradually came to control the entire supply process for certain crops (celery, peas, lettuce, and other vegetables) from the planting to the sale. By 1940, Japanese Americans accounted for roughly half of the total produce business of the major cities on the West Coast.

Building Communities

People of Japanese descent in America—both those who intended to stay permanently in America and those who merely wanted to work for a while and then return to Japan—lived mostly in Hawaii, California, Washington, and Oregon. In Hawaii, where they made up a large percentage of the population (about 39 percent in 1900 and nearly 48 percent by 1920), the Japanese influenced nearly every sector of the economy and settled throughout the

The Japanese business district in Los Angeles, 1907

islands. On the West Coast of the mainland, however, the Japanese made up a much smaller percentage of the population. In 1920, for example, about 110,000 people of Japanese descent lived in California, where they made up about 3 percent of the total population of the state.

Like many minorities, the Japanese of the West Coast states tended to live near one another for companionship and assistance. Neighborhoods known as "Little Tokyos" sprang up in most of the cities of the West Coast. A strong sense of community developed among the Japanese living there.

These communities had numerous crucial issues to face. Especially after the Issei—those who had been born in Japan—began to have children, education became a concern. Schools were set up where these children (the Nisei) could study Japanese culture and language. For Nisei who would later return to Japan and have to enter Japanese public schools, this was a practical course of study. As more and more Japanese-American families decided to stay in the United States, however, an American education became more important. Eventually, Japanese community leaders encouraged families to send their Nisei children to American public schools—where all their classes would be taught in English. Many private Japanese-language schools were available to supplement these basic classes. Especially in Hawaii, it was common for Japanese children to attend an American public school during the day and then go directly to Japanese classes afterwards.

The Japanese immigrants formed organizations so that they could act together to protect their rights. More than 50 local Japanese associations were established in California alone. These small groups merged to form the Japanese Agricultural Association of Southern California and the California Farmers Cooperative, two groups that in turn became associated with the Japanese Association of America

A game of goh *among Japanese Americans in Los Angeles in the 1950s*

(JAA). The JAA, headquartered in San Francisco, was much more than a social club. Because it had many local chapters, it could reach Japanese Americans throughout the United States. The JAA sometimes even acted as a liaison between the Japanese government and the Japanese in America. Another important organization, the Japanese American Citizens League, formed in 1929 and grew into a major influence (especially among the Nisei) just before World War II.

Japanese-language newspapers were a valuable means of communication among the Japanese workers. Especially in the late 19th century, very few of the Japanese in Hawaii or the United States could speak English, much less read it, but they still wanted to keep informed about events beyond their own neighborhoods. Mostly based in California, Japanese-language newspapers started becoming available in the late 1880s. Many had short lives. Others attained wide readership and continued publishing for decades. The *Nichibei Shimbun* (Japanese American News), for example, was founded in San Francisco in 1899 and remained in circulation until 1942.

Picture Brides

In the 1880s and 1890s, most Japanese immigrants were men between the ages of 20 and 40. Until the end of World War I, Japanese men greatly outnumbered Japanese women in the United States—by about three to one. Because of this imbalance, many Japanese men married women from Japan and brought them to the U.S.

A male Japanese immigrant in the United States did not often have the money or the free time to travel to Japan and then return with a bride. Also, any young man who had not yet served in the Japanese military risked being drafted if he returned to Japan and stayed too long. To allow such men to find wives without leaving America, a practice developed that became known as a "picture bride" marriage. This long-distance form of courtship got its name because it often involved an exchange of photographs between a man in the United States and a woman in Japan.

The immigrant would write a letter back home to his parents telling them that he wanted to marry a suitable Japanese woman. The pictures enclosed with these letters were sometimes a little less than honest, portraying the man as either younger or richer than he actually was. He would often ask his parents or other relatives to make a marriage proposal to a young woman from his hometown in Japan. His relatives then made extensive inquiries into the woman's family background, training, manners, and general character. The bride's relatives would then investigate their future son-in-law's family, character, and personal circumstances. If both parties seemed satisfactory, the marriage ceremony would be performed in Japan with the bride in attendance but with the groom's family standing in for him. The groom himself was nearly halfway around the world at the time of his own wedding.

After the marriage ceremony in Japan, the Japanese government would permit the bride to join her new husband in the United States. After finally meeting each other—often at the docks in San Francisco or Seattle—the couple might go through another marriage ceremony in accordance with American customs. Picture-bride marriage seemed strange to many non-Japanese Americans and helped build prejudice against Japanese immigrants. In 1921, the Japanese government announced that it would discontinue issuing passports to picture brides because of American opposition to this practice.

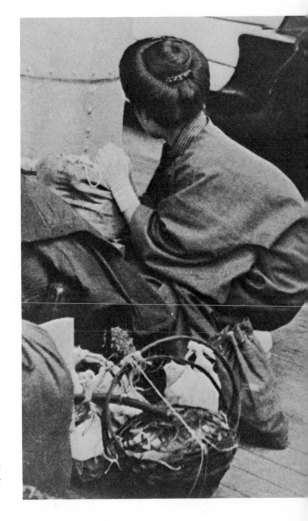

A picture bride newly arrived from Japan waited aboard ship before stepping ashore in California.

3
PREJUDICE AND WAR

Japanese residents of the U.S.-controlled Panama Canal Zone were removed from their homes in 1942.

A Longstanding Problem

From the very beginning of their immigration to the United States, the Japanese were at a disadvantage. In 1790, the U.S. Congress had passed a law stating that only "free white persons" could become naturalized citizens of the United States. This meant that a foreigner who was a slave or nonwhite would forever remain a visitor, no matter how long he or she lived in the United States. The children of this foreigner could become U.S. citizens if they were born within U.S. territory, but an original immigrant who was not both free and white was barred from citizenship.

In 1870, an act of Congress amended this policy somewhat. Persons of African ancestry, the act said, could now be granted U.S. citizenship. This revised law, however, still excluded persons who were neither white nor of African descent. This exclusion worked mostly against people from Asia.

A few immigrants from Japan and other Asian countries managed to gain U.S. citizenship because, in some cases, the law was not strictly enforced. Overall, however, Japanese immigrants—the Issei—were not eligible for citizenship. In 1922, the U.S. Supreme Court supported this point of view by ruling that the Japanese were not white and therefore did not qualify under the law for naturalization. Although the Nisei born in the U.S. were U.S. citizens, the vast majority of Issei were not and never could be.

Exclusionist groups—those that argued for keeping the Japanese out of certain businesses, schools, neighborhoods, towns, or even the entire country—used this situation against the Japanese. The Issei's ineligibility for citizenship provided a weak excuse for the racist hatred that developed against the Japanese in America, especially in California.

The San Francisco School Controversy

Open hostility against Japanese Americans surfaced in San Francisco shortly after the beginning of the 20th century. San Francisco was then governed by Mayor Eugene E. Schmitz and his political boss, Abraham Ruef. After the Schmitz-Ruef administration of San Francisco (1901-1906) was charged with corruption in office, they tried to divert public attention from themselves by blaming many social problems on the Japanese.

Mayor Schmitz had been elected with the support of the Union Labor Party, which objected to competition from immigrant workers, particularly the Japanese. The Union Labor Party claimed that the new immigrants worked for lower wages and were driving other Americans out of their jobs. In response to these complaints, the Japanese government in 1900 restricted the number of passports issued to laborers wishing to come to the United States. Still, many Japanese managed to enter the United States— sometimes via Hawaii, Canada, or Mexico.

Another factor that contributed to the anti-Japanese sentiment in the western states was the outbreak of the Russo-Japanese War in 1904. The rapid success of Japanese military forces in this conflict and the eventual seizure of Korea by Japan made many U.S. citizens fearful of the "Yellow Peril"— an imagined threat by Oriental people to the living standards and power of Western civilization. Fears were expressed that the West Coast would be flooded with a wave of new Japanese immigrants at the end of the Russo-Japanese War. American labor groups were worried that their jobs would be endangered. Finally, in 1905, serious anti-Japanese prejudice surfaced.

Non-Japanese Americans accused the Japanese of forcing shoe-repair shops out of business, of deliberately undercharging for construction work in order to grab most of the business, and of controlling most of the manual laborers on the railroads in California. These charges were false, but many Americans believed them. The *San Francisco Chronicle*, the city's leading newspaper, ran front-page articles on the danger of additional immigration to the U.S. mainland from Japan and Hawaii. The *Chronicle* charged that Japanese Americans were still loyal to the Meiji emperor of Japan and insisted that the immigrant children were crowding other children out of San Francisco classrooms.

With the urging of the *Chronicle*, organized labor in San Francisco began an all-out attack against the Japanese in America. A citywide boycott was started against Japanese merchants; mass meetings were held at which the immigrants were denounced as evil intruders who were undermining the United States. Some outright assaults upon individual immigrants took place. Non-Japanese Americans demanded that the federal government exclude the Japanese from the U.S., and legislators from California introduced such a bill in Congress. President Theodore Roosevelt, however, was greatly opposed to this bill and said that he would veto any law excluding the Japanese, even if it passed Congress unanimously.

Even though newspapers in major West Coast cities ran editorials strongly criticizing Roosevelt, his stern statements killed the hope of the exclusionists for a time. A major disaster, however, was soon to revive anti-Japanese forces in San Francisco.

On April 18, 1906, San Francisco experienced the worst earthquake and fire in its history. More than 10,000 Japanese Americans were driven from their homes by the catastrophe, and they had to find new places to live. Many of these displaced persons moved into neighborhoods that had previously been white enclaves. This put the Japanese into direct contact with many non-Japanese who were racially prejudiced. After the earthquake and fire, San Francisco experienced a major crime wave, which hit the Japanese particularly hard. Japanese stores were looted, and leading Japanese figures were often victims of rock-throwing gangs.

In 1906, the San Francisco school board ruled that Japanese-American students could no longer go to school with students of European descent. The board directed all children of Japanese immigrants to attend a separate "Oriental school" in Chinatown. The Japanese Association of America immediately protested this order. They pointed out, for one thing, that attendance at this special school would be extremely difficult for those Japanese children who lived far from Chinatown. More importantly, however, Japanese

This drawing by San Francisco artist Arthur Lewis shows the destruction wreaked by the 1906 earthquake and fire.

families felt insulted by the board's order. The Japanese government also protested this form of discrimination. President Roosevelt described the board's action as a "wicked absurdity."

Racial prejudice, not overcrowding at the schools, was the motivation for the school board's ruling. Out of a total enrollment of 25,000, there were only 93 Japanese students attending the San Francisco schools. Another false claim widely publicized by the anti-Japanese was that many older Japanese were attending school with much younger children. Actually, there were only two immigrants over 20

years of age attending schools in San Francisco, and they were there to learn English.

Leading educators across the U.S. spoke out against this order by the San Francisco school board. Early in 1907, to settle the matter, President Roosevelt convinced the school board to reverse its decision and cancel the order. As part of the bargain, however, Roosevelt agreed to limit the immigration of Japanese into the United States via Hawaii and other areas outside the states. This agreement was not enough, however, to silence anti-Japanese forces.

The Gentlemen's Agreement and Land Laws

In 1908, after an exchange of diplomatic notes with the United States, the government of Japan even further restricted emigration from their country. According to an understanding called the Gentlemen's Agreement, the Japanese government prohibited the emigration of Japanese laborers. The United States agreed to continue allowing the immigration of skilled Japanese workers, but the flow of people from Japan was greatly reduced.

For a while, the violence against the Japanese in the West Coast states subsided. Another round of trouble, however, awaited the Japanese in America. The success of Japanese farmers was attracting attention in California. Non-Japanese agricultural groups soon demanded that the Japanese not be allowed to acquire farmland. Several fruitgrower associations and the American Legion of California were among those who charged that Japanese Americans threatened the success of white farmers.

The California legislature responded by overwhelmingly passing the Alien Land Law of 1913. This law banned the purchase of farmland by anyone who was not eligible for citizenship. Such wording targeted Japanese immigrants without mentioning them specifically. The law also limited the length of Japanese-held land leases to three years.

The United States government opposed these actions by the state of California. While the California legislature was considering the Alien Land Law, the federal government tried to influence the debate. President Woodrow Wilson sent Secretary of State William Jennings Bryan to California to prevent passage. The legislature, more strongly influenced by anti-Japanese groups, ignored the pleas of federal officials and passed the Alien Land Law.

The Japanese immigrants protested bitterly and charged that they were being denied equal protection of the law as guaranteed in the 14th Amendment to the U.S. Constitution. Their protests, however, were generally ignored in California. Unable to change the law, the Japanese found ways around it. For example, those who had American-born children could buy property in the name of their children, who were American citizens. Most of these loopholes were closed, however, when the California legislature enacted an even stricter Alien Land Law in 1920. The state of Washington followed in 1921 with its own legal restrictions on land ownership by the Japanese. Throughout the West, the 1920s brought ever greater discrimination against the Japanese in America.

The final success of the anti-Japanese forces on the West Coast came when the U.S. Congress passed

Japanese workers in California gathered in 1907 in front of a row of small houses provided for farmhands.

the Immigration Act of 1924. Without mentioning the Japanese by name, this law provided for their total exclusion by refusing entry to aliens ineligible for United States citizenship. President Calvin Coolidge said that if the measure had been openly directed against the Japanese, he would have vetoed it. Coolidge signed the act into law nonetheless. Although the U.S. government still permitted a few Japanese to enter for family reasons or under other unusual circumstances, Japanese immigration to the United States came to a virtual halt.

The Coming of War

In 1931, Japan invaded Manchuria (in what is now northeastern China), drawing a strong protest from the governments of the United States and many other nations. In 1934, Japan withdrew from the League of Nations and scrapped an international treaty limiting the size of the Japanese navy. By 1937, Japan had invaded China. Japanese military actions—including the destruction of the city of Nanking in December 1937 and the sinking of a U.S. gunboat (the *Panay*) by Japanese aircraft—caused anti-Japanese sentiment to mount rapidly in the U.S. Soon the United States government stopped oil shipments to Japan, and relations between the two nations steadily worsened.

The Japanese Americans living in the U.S. became the target of many groups who were nursing old complaints and grievances against them. All of the old arguments—about unfair competition, loyalty to the Japanese emperor, and the supposedly evil influence that the Japanese were exerting upon white children—were brought out and used again. Letters to the editors of West Coast newspapers attacked Japanese Americans as possible spies and saboteurs for the Empire of Japan. Poisonous nonsense began pouring from various organizations that aimed to destroy the Japanese settlements. For example, the following statement was issued in

The USS Shaw exploded during the Japanese raid on Pearl Harbor.

1935 by a Southern California group calling itself the Committee of One Thousand:

> Wherever the Japanese have settled, their nests pollute the communities like the running sores of leprosy. They exist like the yellowed, smoldering discarded butts in an over-full ashtray, vilifying the air with their loathsome smells, filling all who have misfortune to look upon them with a wholesome disgust and a desire to wash.

The attack on Pearl Harbor on December 7, 1941, prompted many non-Japanese groups—including chambers of commerce from large cities, farm groups, American Legion posts, the Native Sons and Daughters of the Golden West, and various fraternal business organizations—to demand that all Japanese Americans be removed from the West Coast. Some non-Japanese claimed that at least 25,000 Japanese-American civilians were actually loyal Japanese soldiers who would help Japanese troops invade the West Coast. Because of the Pearl Harbor attack and the steady advance of Japanese military forces through Southeast Asia and the Pacific during the first months of the war, many U.S. citizens were ready to believe almost any story about Japanese Americans.

One of the most widely believed stories was that the Japanese attack on Pearl Harbor was aided by Japanese Americans living in Hawaii. After the attack, stories were told about how strange lights gave signals to Japanese submarines. Another tale described how the Japanese Americans mowed their crops into the shape of arrows to point Japanese bombers toward Pearl Harbor. Japanese Americans were said to have secret radio transmitters to send reports of American troop movements. Fishing fleets from Hawaii were said to be spying on U.S. naval movements.

Many organizations urged the complete removal of the Japanese from the West Coast to concentration camps for the duration of the war. Other groups advised the government to ship all Japanese Americans back to Japan after the war. Many of these groups encouraged their members to write letters to their congresspersons. Public pressure on legislators did develop, but it was not overwhelming. Overall, federal legislators received fewer letters of protest against the Japanese than against the military draft established by the Selective Service Act of 1940.

Still, the situation was tense. On January 31, 1942, Culbert Olson, the California governor, issued an order revoking the business licenses of 5,000 Japanese aliens. Earl Warren, who was then the attorney general of California (and who would later become chief justice of the U.S. Supreme Court), said that hundreds of Japanese groups

should be disbanded and that all truck farmers who farmed on land near naval, army, or air force installations should be removed. Warren also remarked, in defense of such racist actions, that one could not tell the difference between a good Japanese American and a bad one. Governor Arthur B. Langlie of Washington and Governor Charles A. Sprague of Oregon advised that they were keeping close watch on the situation in their states. Washington and Oregon combined, however, had fewer than 30,000 Japanese Americans at this time, and the tension was considerably lower there than in California.

Recognizing the threat to them, Japanese Americans tried to prove their loyalty to the United States. One group of Japanese Americans in Santa Ana, California, pledged funds to purchase an antiaircraft gun for the government's use in war. (An antiaircraft gun at that time cost approximately $50,000.)

The U.S. House of Representatives set up a committee to investigate "un-American activities" and placed an anti-Japanese legislator, Martin Dies of Texas, at the head of the committee. On February 4, 1942, the Dies Committee announced that it would publish a "yellow paper" to disclose that more than 150,000 Japanese Americans belonged to a spy ring. Martin

Dies warned, "The West Coast is in for a tragedy that will make Pearl Harbor sink into insignificance." Four days later, the Dies Committee recommended that all Japanese be moved from the coast. The "yellow paper," however, was never published, and no evidence of the alleged spy ring was ever made public.

Anti-Japanese groups, in an effort to force the removal of Japanese Americans from the West Coast, directed much of their lobbying toward two federal agencies, the Department of

Justice and the Department of War. Radio commentators and newspaper writers protested to the Department of Justice that its failure to act would create another "Pearl Harbor" on the West Coast. The Department of Justice stated that it was unequipped to handle any large-scale movements of people over considerable distances. This left the matter up to the War Department.

On February 19, 1942, President Franklin D. Roosevelt signed Executive Order 9066, a directive that authorized the Secretary of War to move people out of militarily strategic territory. The War Department then delegated this authority to General John L. DeWitt, who was in charge of the Western Defense Command and the Fourth Army. DeWitt agreed with those who feared the Japanese Americans, an attitude that is demonstrated by remarks he made later (in 1943) to the House Naval Affairs Committee:

> I don't want any of them [persons of Japanese ancestry] here. They are a dangerous element. ...It makes no difference whether he is an American citizen, he is still a Japanese. You needn't worry about the Italians at all except in certain cases. Also, the same for the Germans except in individual cases. But we must worry about the Japanese all the time until he is wiped off the map.

The War Department based its final decision to evacuate the Japanese on the general's insistence that it was a matter of military necessity. The administration of the evacuation process, however, was conducted by a new civilian agency, the War Relocation Authority (WRA). The first head of the WRA was Milton Eisenhower (a brother of General Dwight D. Eisenhower), who was later replaced by Dillon S. Myer.

Evacuation

The removal authorized by Executive Order 9066 was called evacuation, a forced displacement that affected about 110,000 Japanese Americans living in California, Oregon, and Washington. Approximately 10,000 Japanese Americans from other states and territories were also affected. Families of Japanese descent—American citizens and noncitizens alike—were uprooted from their homes and placed in concentration camps. In Hawaii, however, where people of Japanese ancestry were even more numerous and where the danger of Japanese invasion had already been highlighted by the attack on Pearl Harbor, no substantial evacuation was ordered. The Hawaiian economy depended so greatly on the Japanese that evacuation could have meant economic collapse.

The military authorities enforcing the evacuation often moved Japanese families out of their residences and businesses with less than 48 hours' notice. In their haste, many Japanese businesspersons and homeowners had to sell their property for only a small fraction—perhaps as little as 10 to 15 percent—of its true value. Many farmers had to leave their crops standing in the fields and sell their farm equipment for only a few dollars. Non-Japanese Americans who had complained about unfair competition from Japanese farmers found themselves able to buy out their Japanese competitors at incredibly low prices.

Although the federal government set aside warehouses in which evacuees could store some of their personal belongings, most of these warehouses were eventually broken into. Furniture, sewing machines, ovens, and other items were stolen or damaged,

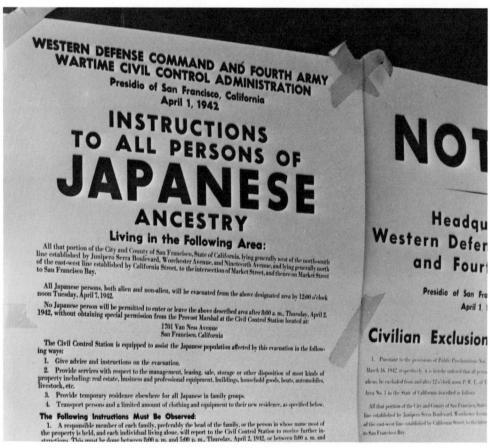

One of the many evacuation orders posted in the western U.S.

A mound of baggage represented the dismantled households of Japanese Americans forced out of their homes. These San Francisco residents were removed from the city on April 29, 1942.

but no one was ever prosecuted for stealing or vandalizing Japanese-American property. Some Japanese suspected that their property would not be safe in government warehouses and signed over control of it to a non-Japanese American for safekeeping during the war. Some of these whites simply sold the property and kept the money. Such treachery added insult to the material losses that interned Japanese Americans suffered.

Relocation Centers

Before dawn on March 24, 1942, about 500 Japanese Americans assembled near the Rose Bowl stadium in Pasadena, California, and started a 200-mile (about 320-kilometer) drive to Owens Valley, California. These 500 people had volunteered to make a camp in Owens Valley livable for other Japanese Americans who were to follow shortly. Upon their arrival, the

The Mochida family of Hayward, California, left for an internment camp on May 8, 1942. Most of the children wore the identification tags required by federal regulations.

volunteers found a desolate, wind-swept camp with only 38 prefabricated barracks, a temporary field hospital, a small mess hall, and an administration office. In the next seven weeks, the volunteers not only erected additional facilities but also organized baseball teams, a dance orchestra, and regular religious services.

The Owens Valley Center was just one of 16 temporary camps—sometimes called assembly centers—that were the first stop for the Japanese Americans who were to be resettled. Some of these assembly centers were hastily pieced together at racetracks; others were at fairgrounds or other publicly owned open spaces. Privacy, comfort, and hygienic facilities were hard to come by at these centers—

which were very temporary. By the end of October 1942, 15 of these short-lived boom towns had become ghost towns. (The Owens Valley Assembly Center was converted to a sturdier camp and was renamed Manzanar.) The Japanese Americans had been moved to other camps—a total of 10, including Manzanar—known sometimes as relocation centers and sometimes as internment camps.

Relocation centers were located on public land in desolate areas such as deserts and swamps. (The federal government hoped to use camp residents as laborers to improve the land.) Even though the relocation centers were more habitable than the temporary assembly centers, they were far from luxurious. Each family was

A dusty windstorm swept through the Manzanar Relocation Center in California on July 3, 1942.

allotted its own living unit, but each family unit was not much more than a large room. These rooms were subdivisions of long, barracks-style buildings. Residents of the internment camps lived very much like prisoners. Except when they were assigned to outside work details, the Japanese Americans had to stay inside the camps. Armed guards in watchtowers made sure that they did.

Concentrating several thousand people in a camp with crowded living conditions kept tempers at the boiling point. Rifts developed within the interned communities. Some of the Issei taunted the Nisei about the "advantages" of their U.S. citizenship. In December 1942, Fred Tayama, a leader of the Japanese American Citizens League at the Manzanar camp, was severely beaten. When several residents who had been openly critical of the U.S. government were arrested for the beating, trouble worsened. Ralph P. Merritt, a camp director at Manzanar, reported that riots had broken out within the Japanese community, and two residents of the camp were killed when authorities put down the uprising.

As hard as camp life was, most of the interned population did their best to make it more tolerable. The adults elected camp councils to present a strong voice in dealing with government authorities. By organizing recreational activities, printing camp newspapers, and encouraging internees to support one another, community leaders among the Japanese tried to soften the blow of internment.

A Different War

Japanese-American members of the U.S. military were in a particularly odd position when the United States and Japan went to war. Despite clear records of honorable service, these soldiers found their loyalty questioned simply because of their ancestry. Some soldiers were stripped of all real responsibility. Others were removed from their usual assignments and transferred to military bases far from the West Coast. Even though the United States needed as many military recruits as it could get, official policy prevented Japanese-American soldiers from going into combat.

In the spring of 1943, the government changed its policy—but only after groups of Japanese-American soldiers had petitioned President Franklin D. Roosevelt to let them see

action. With an initial goal of enlisting 1,500 soldiers, the government asked for Japanese-American volunteers for combat. In Hawaii alone, more than 9,500 men signed up for combat duty. In March 1943, 2,645 were inducted into the U.S. Army in Honolulu, and more than 1,000 Japanese Americans in relocation centers in the U.S. also volunteered for combat duty. Two especially well-known Japanese-American units were formed during World War II, the 100th Infantry Battalion and the 442nd Regimental Combat Team.

The 100th Infantry Battalion

After the Pearl Harbor attack, the Japanese-American members of the Hawaiian National Guard were segregated into a separate group. They were later sent to the U.S. mainland, where they became the heart of the 100th Infantry Battalion. First known as the Hawaiian Provisional Battalion, this group arrived at Camp McCoy in Wisconsin early in June 1942. The unit later moved to Shelby, Mississippi, where it continued its training until August 1943.

The 100th was assigned to part of the 34th Division and arrived in Italy in September of 1943. From September 1943 until February 1944, the 100th Infantry Battalion was in constant action, including the landing at Salerno (on the island of Sicily) and the heavy

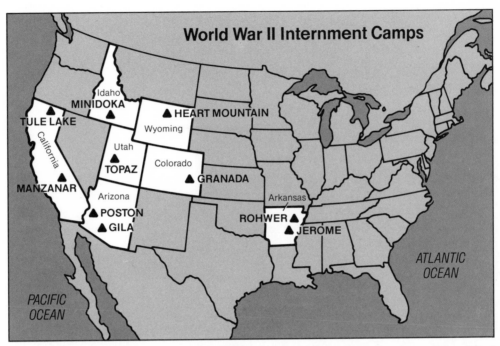

World War II Internment Camps

The War Relocation Authority administered internment camps in seven states. Most camps were in the western United States.

fighting that took place there. After nearly six months of action in the Italian campaign, the Japanese Americans of the 100th Battalion had suffered almost 600 casualties.

The 442nd Regimental Combat Team

When the 442nd Regimental Combat Team arrived in Italy in June of 1944, it absorbed the 100th Infantry Battalion into its ranks—a happy reunion with friends or relatives for many of the Japanese-American soldiers. The 100th Infantry Battalion, after having marched through the city of Pisa in northern Italy, continued its operations as the U.S. Army crossed the Arno River. Subsequently, the 100th Infantry was pulled back from the front lines for a month's rest, and in September 1944 it joined the Seventh Army in the invasion of France from the south.

During this time, the 442nd Regimental Combat Team performed what was probably its most heroic action—the rescue of the famous Lost Battalion of the 36th Texas Division of the U.S. Army. The Lost Battalion had been

In July of 1944, victorious Japanese-American troops from Hawaii rode through the ruins of Leghorn, Italy.

isolated behind German lines for one week, and the German high command was determined that the battalion would not be rescued, no matter what the cost might be. Since the 100th and 3rd battalions of the 442nd Regimental Combat Team were the freshest troops in the Seventh Army, they were ordered to rescue the Lost Battalion. During this engagement, the 442nd lost more soldiers than in any of its other operations during the entire war. Some units lost 60 percent of their troops, and casualties ran even higher in some rifle companies. The fighting was so heavy that many companies had only 30 to 40 soldiers left, and

one company was down to fewer than 10. Some companies and platoons operated without their regular officers, who had been killed or wounded; the noncommissioned officers took command and continued the battle. After nearly six days of combat, the 442nd Regimental Combat Team rescued the Lost Battalion.

In March 1945, the Japanese-American units joined the 92nd Division and fought in Italy for the rest of the war. During this campaign, Sadao S. Munemori earned the Congressional Medal of Honor.

Munemori—born in Los Angeles, California—volunteered as a member of the 100th Infantry Battalion. On April 5, 1945, near Seravezza, Italy, he gave his life in a heroic gesture. The army citation awarded in his memory best describes his contributions:

> He fought with great gallantry and intrepidity near Seravezza, Italy. When his unit was pinned down by grazing fire from the enemy's strong mountain defense and command of the squad devolved on him with the wounding of its regular leader, he made frontal, one-man attacks through direct fire and knocked out two machine guns with grenades. Withdrawing under murderous fire and showers of grenades from other enemy emplacements, he had nearly reached a shell crater occupied by two of his men when an unexploded grenade bounced on his helmet and rolled toward his helpless comrades. He arose in withering fire, dived for the missile and smothered its blast with his body. By his swift supremely heroic action Private Munemori saved two of his men at the cost of his own life and did much to clear the path for his company's victorious advance.

Private Sadao S. Munemori

The 442nd returned to the U.S. on July 2, 1946. On July 16, they were awarded a distinguished honor by the president of the U.S., Harry S. Truman. After reviewing the troops, President Truman gave the 442nd Regimental

Teruo Temono and other Nisei worked as translators in Tokyo for the U.S. administration of Japan just after the war.

Combat Team the Presidential Distinguished Unit Citation. President Truman's address to the unit included the following praise:

> You fought for the free nations of the world along with the rest of us. I congratulate you for that, and I can't tell you how very much I appreciate the privilege of being able to show you just how much…America thinks of what you have done. You are now on your way home. You fought not only the enemy, but you fought prejudice, and you have won. Keep up that fight, and we continue to win—to make this great Republic stand for just what the Constitution says it stands for: the welfare of all the people all the time.

The 442nd received seven Presidential Unit Citations for outstanding operations and brilliant tactics during their months in combat in Italy and France. The individual members of the 442nd Regimental Combat Team and the 100th Infantry Battalion received more than 5,940 awards and medals from the U.S. government in addition to awards that individual members received from the governments of France and Italy.

Civilian Contributions

While Japanese-American soldiers were achieving success and acclaim in Europe, other Japanese Americans were doing their share toward the nation's war effort. The U.S. military soon found that it needed many interpreters in the Pacific. Since there were few non-Japanese Americans who could speak or read the Japanese language, the army accepted Nisei interpreters on a trial basis. These Nisei soon proved invaluable to the U.S. armed forces in the Pacific and gained much useful information questioning prisoners of war. Although Issei volunteers were not used as interpreters near combat zones, many became instructors at the special language schools established by the U.S. armed forces to train Japanese interpreters.

Also behind the lines, other Japanese-American women and men rolled bandages and prepared medical kits for the Red Cross. War-bond drives to raise money for the U.S. war effort were enthusiastically supported in Japanese communities.

The End of Internment

The Japanese Americans in the relocation centers tried to adapt to their internment, but they were eager to be free. They had some support among non-Japanese Americans. Some officials of private colleges in the eastern United States offered scholarships to bright students in the camps and convinced camp authorities to release these students. The work done by Japanese crews proved very valuable, and it became more common for work crews—under close supervision—to be allowed outside the camps.

In 1944, the government relaxed some of the restrictions on the Japanese Americans in the relocation centers. Since the war was still in progress, they were not permitted to return to the West Coast, but some were allowed to move to the Midwest. They were not always welcomed in their new communities, but anti-Japanese sentiment was not as strong further east as it had been in the western states. The U.S. Supreme Court ruled in December 1944 that loyal Americans of Japanese descent could not be held against their will in internment camps. Soon afterwards, the War Relocation Authority announced that all the camps would be closed by the end of 1945.

When the last relocation center had been closed, many Japanese Americans settled in areas far from the West Coast. Thousands settled in the Midwest—nearly 10,000 settled in Chicago—and others moved their families to New York and other eastern states. About one-third of the families decided to return to their old homes on the West Coast, and after 1946 there was a gradual shift back to the West—to California in particular.

After the War

Even after internment ended and a peace treaty was signed with Japan, Japanese Americans faced difficulties because of their ancestry. Not until 1952, for example, did California cancel the laws restricting land ownership by Japanese Americans. Old prejudices and hatreds still existed on the West Coast, and some whites attacked Japanese Americans. Furthermore, the damage caused by internment could not be quickly corrected.

The total number of Japanese Americans interned at one time or another during the war years came to about 120,000. Their unjust imprisonment interrupted their lives and caused them to lose their homes, their businesses, their farms, and most of their possessions.

The U.S. Congress created the Evacuation Claims Commission and directed the attorney general of the U.S. to reimburse Japanese Americans for damages and property loss caused by relocation. Although the commission, which began processing claims in 1948, arranged for some compensation to be paid to former internees, nearly all of the relocated Japanese Americans lost far more than the government repaid. By 1958, the government had paid out only $38 million—probably less than 15 percent of the actual losses sustained by internees.

Former internees who wanted to file a claim often had difficulty gathering evidence to support it. Many of the evacuees had lost the titles and deeds to their property. Others could not document the value of their personal property. There was no accurate way to determine how much income families had lost during the war years. A system that based claim payments on provable losses could never come close to compensating former internees. Furthermore, the Japanese Americans unjustly imprisoned during the war had suffered insult as well as loss. Many Americans—Japanese and non-Japanese alike—thought the government owed the former internees not just money but also an apology.

A major step forward came with the Civil Liberties Act of 1988. After passage of the act, President Ronald Reagan formally apologized, on behalf of the government of the United States, to the former internees and their descendants. The act also initiated an entirely new mechanism for partially compensating Japanese Americans for their losses that were due to internment.

The 1988 Civil Liberties Act ordered the Civil Rights Division of the Department of Justice to draw up a list of all former internees who were still alive on August 10, 1988 (the day the law went into effect). Each of these persons would be issued a check for $20,000 – an amount known as a redress payment. If a former internee was alive on that date but died before a check could be issued, the redress payment would go to his or her heirs.

If an eligible Japanese American died without leaving heirs, the $20,000 would be paid into the Civil Liberties Public Education Fund, a public source of money for programs to educate Americans about the internment.

The first redress payment check was formally presented on October 9, 1990, to Mamoru Eto, a former internee who was 107 years old at the time he received his check. In the 1988 Civil Liberties Act, Congress had authorized a total of $1.25 billion dollars for redress payments – enough for payments to 62,500 Japanese Americans. Officials at the Department of Justice,

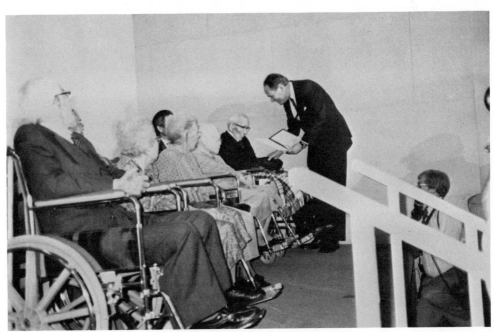

U.S. Attorney General Dick Thornburgh presented the first redress check and an official apology to 107-year-old Rev. Mamoru Eto in October 1990.

At a Japanese-owned Toyota automobile plant in Kentucky, Americans and Japanese cooperated in inaugurating a new research facility.

however, expected that up to 65,000 payments might have to be made and that Congress would have to appropriate more money to meet this obligation.

Although many Japanese Americans lost far more in internment than they recovered in redress payments, most former internees and their descendants felt a sense of victory with the passage of the 1988 act. To many, the government's admission that internment was a mistake meant a great deal. It affirmed the loyalty of Japanese Americans during World War II and formally rejected the notion that their ancestry made them somehow less American than their neighbors.

New Contact with Japan

Although the overwhelming majority of Japanese Americans are descended from immigrants who came to the U.S. before 1924, immigration from Japan has continued. Through the 1980s, about 4,000 immigrants a year came to the United States from Japan.

Besides these immigrants, who have come with the intention of staying in the United States, many Japanese have come to the United States to work temporarily. Increased Japanese influence in U.S. manufacturing and business has brought an influx of Japanese executives, consultants, and managers. Although these workers intend to return to Japan, their contact with the United States has shaped U.S. business practices. Their presence is also one factor in an increasing American familiarity with elements of Japanese culture, such as sushi (a buffet-style meal involving rice cakes and various toppings) and karaoke lounges (where customers are encouraged to take the stage and sing along to prerecorded music). In far more subtle ways, however—and for a very long time—the United States has been influenced by the Japanese who have made their homes in America.

With numerous Japanese legislators in attendance, President Ronald Reagan signed the 1988 Civil Liberties Act into law.

4
CONTRIBUTIONS TO AMERICAN LIFE

Ellison Onizuka, the first Japanese-American astronaut, died in the explosion of the space shuttle **Challenger** *in 1986.*

Government and Public Affairs

The role of Japanese Americans in government has been strong. Especially in Hawaii and California, many Japanese Americans have served as mayors, city councilpersons, state legislators, and other local and state officeholders. Hawaii's governor from 1974 to 1986 was George Ariyoshi, a Japanese American. Other Japanese-American political leaders have held important national offices.

Senator Daniel Ken Inouye of Hawaii, who had lost an arm while fighting for the United States in World War II, started his political career in the Hawaiian Territorial House of Representatives in 1952. When the new state of Hawaii sent its first congresspersons to the U.S. House of Representatives in 1959, Inouye was among them. He was elected to the U.S. Senate in 1962 and played a major role in the

Senator Daniel K. Inouye served in the 442nd Regimental Combat Team during World War II. "Go for broke," the slogan on the flag in the background, was the unit's motto.

Japanese-American soldiers were sidelined, but they petitioned President Roosevelt to let them see action. As a member of the 100th Infantry Battalion, he fought in Italy and was wounded twice. During the 1950s, Matsunaga was a member of the Hawaiian Territorial Legislature, of which he became majority leader in 1959. Matsunaga first won election to the U.S. House of Representatives in 1962 and to the U.S. Senate in 1976. Senator Matsunaga died in April 1990, less than

Senate's investigation of the Watergate affair in the early 1970s. He also campaigned vigorously to win redress payments for Japanese Americans who had been interned during World War II.

Senator Spark Masayuki Matsunaga, another Hawaiian member of the U.S. Senate, also pushed for the 1988 legislation that mandated redress payments. Born in Kauai, Hawaii, in 1916, he had joined the U.S. Army before Japan's attack on Pearl Harbor in 1941. When war came, Matsunaga and other

Spark M. Matsunaga

Patricia Saiki

half a year before Japanese Americans began to receive the redress payments he had fought hard to legislate.

Two politically prominent Japanese-American women from Hawaii have served in the U.S. House of Representatives. Patricia Saiki, a Republican, started her political career in Hawaii's state legislature and then went to Washington, D.C., in 1986 to serve in Congress. She also was a member of the U.S. delegation to the funeral of Japan's Emperor Hirohito in 1989. In 1990, she ran for election to the U.S. Senate instead of for reelection to the House of Representatives, but she lost to Daniel K. Akaka.

Patsy Takemoto Mink served in the Hawaiian legislature through much of the 1950s and in 1964 was elected to the U.S. House of Representatives, in which she served through 1977. After she left Congress, she worked for about a year in the executive branch of government as assistant secretary of state for oceans and international environmental and scientific affairs. After returning to Hawaii, she served as a member of the Honolulu City Council from 1983 to 1987. In 1990, Mink returned to her congressional career by winning reelection to the U.S. House of Representatives.

Japanese Americans have also contributed greatly to California's political leadership. Samuel I. Hayakawa, a well-known scholar and a former president of San Francisco State College, entered politics and was one of the

U.S. Senate's most colorful conservative members from 1977 to 1983. Norman Yoshio Mineta began his political career in the government of his hometown, San Jose, California. He served as San Jose's mayor from 1971 until 1975, when he won a seat in the U.S. House of Representatives. Another Japanese-American leader from California—Robert Takeo Matsui of Sacramento—was elected to the U.S. House of Representatives in 1979. Mineta and Matsui, both active in the drive for

redress payments to former internees, were on hand in October 1990 at the formal presentation of the first redress-payment check.

Astronaut Ellison S. Onizuka, the first Japanese American to travel in space, was born in Kealakekua, Hawaii, in 1946. After earning degrees in aerospace engineering, Onizuka joined the National Aeronautics and Space Administration (NASA) in 1978. His first spaceflight came in 1985, when he participated in a classified military mission aboard the shuttle *Discovery*. In the following year, tragedy struck: Lieutenant Colonel Ellison S. Onizuka was aboard the shuttle *Challenger* when it exploded in flight in 1986.

Business

Businesspersons were among the first Japanese immigrants to Hawaii and the United States in the late 19th century. Ever since those early days, Japanese leadership in the business community has continued.

Cynthia Mayeda, a Japanese American from Minnesota, became a leader in the field of business contributions to charitable organizations. The Dayton Hudson Corporation, which owns department stores and other retail outlets, distributes its charitable contributions through an organization known as the Dayton Hudson Foundation. As chairperson of the Dayton Hudson Foundation in the 1990s,

Rep. Robert T. Matsui

Cynthia Mayeda

Mayeda led the organization through a controversy over contributions to a family-planning group.

Hiraoki (Rocky) Aoki, born in 1940 in Japan, established one of the most successful restaurant chains in the United States. The Benihana National Corporation, based in Florida, was founded by Aoki to coordinate the operations of the many Benihana Japanese steakhouses throughout the United States. Aoki's many other interests included hot-air ballooning, speedboat racing, and arranging sports events—especially those that would forge links between Japan and the United States.

Science, Education, and Scholarship

Many Japanese Americans have been at the forefront of research and teaching in the United States. Professor Henry Tatsumi, a specialist on the Japanese language, contributed greatly to the U.S. effort in World War II by instructing officers of the United States Navy at the Japanese language school located in Boulder, Colorado. Professor John Maki, an expert on the government and politics of Japan, is another scholar of note. Although Samuel I. Hayakawa is best known as a senator, he also is well-known among linguists for his writings about semantics (the study of meaning in language).

Another Japanese-American researcher who built strong reputations in diverse fields is Dr. Thomas Tsunetomi Noguchi. Born in Fukuoka, Japan, in 1927, Noguchi came to the United States in 1952. A specialist in forensic pathology (a field best known for investigating the medical circumstances surrounding crimes), Noguchi began working with the Los Angeles County coroner's office in 1961 and headed that office from 1967 to 1982. Noguchi had a role in several high-profile cases—such as the investigations into Marilyn Monroe's death, Robert F. Kennedy's assassination, and the murders for which Charles Manson was convicted. After becoming a professor of forensic pathology at University of Southern California Medical Center in 1982, Noguchi wrote two nonfiction accounts of his experiences as a coroner. He also authored two murder-mystery novels, *Unnatural Causes* (1988) and *Physical Evidence* (1990).

In 1989, a young Japanese-American scholar working for the United States Department of State became notable for writing an article entitled "The End of History?" In this influential piece, Francis Fukuyama—trained at Cornell, Yale, and Harvard in literature, philosophy, and political science—analyzed the historical significance of the many political changes in Eastern Europe during the late 1980s.

Architecture, Art, and Literature

The distinguished Japanese-American architect Minoru Yamasaki has designed some of the most prominent structures in the United States and other nations. Yamasaki, born in

Minoru Yamasaki

Seattle in 1912, graduated from the University of Washington in 1934 and continued his studies at New York University. Among his many works are the Reynolds Metals Company building in Detroit, the Oberlin College Music Conservatory in Ohio, the Dhahran International Airport terminal in Dhahran, Saudi Arabia, and the Northwestern National Life Insurance Company building in Minneapolis. Yamasaki also designed the Woodrow Wilson School of Public and International Affairs for Princeton University. By far his most prominent achievement, however, is the two-towered World Trade Center in New York City. In 1956, Yamasaki received the First Honor Award from the American Institution of Architects. Yamasaki died in 1986 at Birmingham, Michigan.

The noted sculptor Isamu Noguchi was born in Los Angeles in 1904, attended Columbia University in New York, and studied in various parts of the world, including Paris and China. Some of his larger works stand in Great Britain and Mexico, but he is probably best known for the relief sculpture he created for the Associated Press building in Rockefeller Center in New York City. He also designed works for the New York World's Fair in 1939 and had one-artist shows in nearly every major art gallery in the United States. In 1964, Noguchi was called in as a consultant for the design of John F. Kennedy's tomb in Arlington National Cemetery in Arlington, Virginia.

Noguchi remained active even into his later years and maintained a studio on Long Island in New York until his death in 1988.

Among many other Japanese Americans prominent in the arts is Yasuo Kunioshi, a painter associated with the Ash Can School, a group of realist painters in New York early in the 20th century.

In literature, Karen Tei Yamashita is known for her fresh, fantasy-oriented literary style. Born in Gardena, California, Yamashita has studied in Japan and done historical research in Brazil,

Karen Tei Yamashita

Isamu Noguchi with the award-winning bronze plaque he designed for the Associated Press building in New York City, 1938

where she lived for 10 years in the late 1970s and early 1980s. Many of the plays she has written have been staged in the Los Angeles area, and she has written many highly acclaimed short stories. In 1979, Yamashita won the James Clavell American-Japanese Short Story Contest, and in 1990 she published her first novel, *Through the Arc of the Rain Forest*.

Japanese Americans have also been prominent in dance and choreography. Sono Osato, a half-Japanese American born in Nebraska in 1919, is one example. As a child, she lived in several cities in France and the United States and studied ballet. An accomplished dancer at an early age, she was dancing with the famous Ballet Russe of Paris by the time she was 15 years old.

Music

Seiji Ozawa, one of the most prominent symphony conductors in the world, was born in Japan in 1935 and left for Europe in 1959 to study conducting. Leonard Bernstein of the New York Philharmonic Orchestra saw Ozawa in Europe and, impressed by Ozawa's abilities, named him assistant conductor of the New York Philharmonic for the 1961-62 season. From 1965 to 1969, Ozawa was the conductor of the Toronto Symphony, and in 1968 he was named conductor and musical director of the San Francisco Symphony Orchestra. Ozawa has appeared as guest conductor for many of the best symphony orchestras in the United States and Europe during breaks from his regular duties as musical director of the Boston Symphony Orchestra.

Yoko Ono, a musician and artist, was born in Tokyo in 1933 and came to the United States with her parents—her father was a banker doing business in the U.S.—in 1951. After her parents returned to Japan, she stayed in the United States and began a career as an artist. She and the other artists with whom she associated were unconventional, working with unusual materials and subjects. She eventually met John Lennon of the Beatles, whom she married in 1969. Ono and Lennon became well known for their musical collaborations but even more for their efforts to promote world peace. After

Seiji Ozawa

Yoko Ono and John Lennon

Lennon was murdered in 1980, Ono continued to record music and create art, but she devoted most of her energy—and her considerable fortune—to supporting efforts toward peace.

Sports and Entertainment

Japanese Americans have also made their mark in the field of athletics. Makoto Sakamoto, then a high school student, led the U.S. men's gymnastic squad in the Tokyo Olympics in 1964. Tommy Kono, a health-food salesperson from Hawaii, competed in various weight-lifting contests for over 15 years. He broke 26 world records and won eight world titles and eight national titles. He won Olympic weight-lifting titles for the United States in 1952 and 1956.

Japanese-American actors have been prominent in American film and television for many decades. Sessue Hayakawa (1889-1973) was born in Japan and immigrated to the United States before the First World War. He was nominated in 1957 for an Academy Award as best supporting actor for his work in *The Bridge on the River Kwai*, the film for which he is best known. Miyoshi Umeki won an Academy Award as best supporting actress for her role in the 1957 film *Sayonara*. Jack Soo (1915-1979) was a Japanese-American television actor who played Nick

Tommy Kono

Yemana in the situation comedy *Barney Miller*.

Perhaps the most widely familiar Japanese-American actor is Noriyuki (Pat) Morita. During the 1970s, Morita played a restaurant owner named Arnold in the comedy series *Happy Days*. He then went on to star in one of the biggest film hits of 1984, *The Karate Kid*, and was nominated for an Academy Award as best supporting actor for his role as a wise teacher in that film. He also starred in the 1986 sequel, *The Karate Kid, Part II*.

The victims of some of the most systematic discrimination ever practiced by the United States government, the Japanese Americans have bounced back with dignity. Ever since they first began moving to the United States and Hawaii in the late 19th century, the Japanese have been renowned for their exceptional talent and their perseverance. Their achievements have greatly enhanced American life and have been a source of pride to generation after generation of the Japanese in America.

Sessue Hayakawa (right) *with Alec Guinness in* **The Bridge on the River Kwai**

The Santa Anita racetrack in Arcadia, California, served as a temporary school for interned Japanese-American schoolchildren in 1942.

INDEX

Alaska, Japanese in, 12
alien land laws, 28, 44
Aoki, Hiraoki, 52
Ariyoshi, George, 48

California, Japanese in, 12, 15-16, 18, 19-20, 21, 22, 25, 26, 28, 31, 32, 33, 40, 44, 47, 49, 50, 52, 53
Camp McCoy, Wisconsin, 38
Chinese Exclusion Act, 15
citizenship for Japanese in U.S., 24-25
Civil Liberties Act (1988), 44-46, 47
commerce, Japanese involvement in, 18-19
contract laborers, 11-13, 14, 19

DeWitt, John L., 32, 33
Dies, Martin, 32-33

Edo Treaty, 9
education of Japanese in U.S., 13, 20-21, 60
Eisenhower, Milton, 33
emigration companies, 11-12
evacuation, policy of, 33-35, 60
Evacuation Claims Commission, 43-44
Executive Order 9066, 33

farming by Japanese in United States, 11, 12, 14-16, 28, 34
fishing, 17-18
442nd Regimental Combat Team, 38, 39-40, 41-43
Fukuyama, Francis, 53

Gentlemen's Agreement, 28

Hawaii, Japanese in, 7, 8, 11, 12, 15, 19, 21, 22, 31, 33, 38, 47, 48-49, 50, 56
Hayakawa, Samuel I., 50-51, 52
Hayakawa, Sessue, 58, 59

immigration of Japanese to U.S., restrictions on, 7, 13, 25, 27, 28
Immigration Act of 1924, 8, 29
Inouye, Daniel K., 48-49
internment camps: closing of, 43-44; conditions in, 35-38, 60; establishment of, 35-36; location of, 39
Issei, 8, 20, 25, 37, 43

Japan: industrialization of, 9-10, 11; isolation of, 43-44; military expansion by, 10, 25, 29;
Japanese American Citizens League, 22, 37
Japanese Association of America, 21-22

Kanagawa, Treaty of, 9
Kono, Tommy, 58
Kunioshi, Yasuo, 54

land ownership by Japanese in U.S.,15-16, 28-29, 44
Little Tokyos, 20

Maki, John, 52
Manzanar internment camp, 36, 37-38
Matsui, Robert T., 51
Matsunaga, Spark M., 49-50
Mayeda, Cynthia, 51-52
Meiji period, 9-10, 13
Meiji, Emperor, 9, 26
Merritt, Ralph P., 37
Mineta, Norman Y., 51
Mink, Patsy T., 50
Morita, Noriyuki (Pat), 59
Munemori, Sadao S., 40-41
Myer, Dillon S., 33

Nakahama, Manjiro, 7
Nisei, 8, 20, 21, 22, 25, 37, 43
Noguchi, Isamu, 54, 55
Noguchi, Thomas T., 52-53

Olson, Culbert, 31
100th Infantry Battalion, 38-39, 40, 41, 43, 48
Onizuka, Ellison S., 48, 51
Ono, Yoko, 56-58
Oregon, Japanese in, 12, 19, 32, 33
Osato, Sono, 55
Owens Valley Assembly Center, 35-36
Ozawa, Seiji, 56

Panay, sinking of, 30
Pearl Harbor, Hawaii, attack on, 30, 31, 33, 38, 48

Perry, Matthew C., 8-9
picture brides, 22-23
population statistics for Japanese immigrants, 6-7, 19-20
prejudice against Japanese, 15, 23, 24-25, 26, 27, 42, 44

Reagan, Ronald, 44
redress payments, 45-46, 48, 49, 50
relocation centers. *See* internment camps.
Roosevelt, Franklin D., 33, 38, 48
Roosevelt, Theodore, 26, 27
Ruef, Abraham, 25
Russo-Japanese War, 10, 25

Saiki, Patricia, 50
Sakamoto, Makoto, 58
San Francisco, California: earthquake in (1906), 26, 27; Japanese community in, 22, 23, 25-27; school policy in, 25-27
San Francisco Chronicle, 25-26
Sansei, 8

Schmitz, Eugene, 25
Soo, Jack, 58-59
students, Japanese, in U.S., 13, 15, 26, 27, 43

Tatsumi, Henry, 51
Tayama, Fred, 37
Truman, Harry S., 41-42

Umeki, Miyoshi, 58

Vacaville, California, 16-17

War Relocation Authority, 33, 34, 43-44
Warren, Earl, 31-32
Washington (state), Japanese in, 12, 19, 28, 32, 33
World War II: buildup to, 28-29; Japanese-American civilian contributions to, 43; Japanese-American soldiers in, 38-43;

Yamasaki, Minoru, 53-54
Yamashita, Karen Tei, 54-55
Yonsei, 7

ACKNOWLEDGMENTS The photographs in this book are reproduced through the courtesy of: pp. 2, 34, 35, War Relocation Authority; p. 6, Gloria Kumagai; pp. 9, 10, 27, Library of Congress; pp. 12, 19, Public Archives, State of Hawaii; pp. 14, 18, 20, 21, 29, Toyo Miyatake, Los Angeles, 1907 Japanese Yearbook; p. 16, Hawaii Visitors Bureau Photo; pp. 22, 63, California State Library; pp. 30, 36, 37, National Archives; pp. 32, 40, 41, 42, 60, U.S. Army Photograph; p. 45, Japanese American Citizens League; p. 46, Toyota Motor Manufacturing USA, Inc.; p. 47, Reagan Presidential Library; p. 48, National Aeronautics and Space Administration; p. 49 left, Sen. Daniel K. Inouye; p. 49 right, Office of Sen. Spark M. Matsunaga; p. 50, Patricia Saiki; p. 51, Robert T. Matsui; p. 52, Dayton Hudson Corporation; p. 53, Taro Yamasaki and Daniel Bartush; p. 54, Walker Art Center; p. 55, Isamu Noguchi; p. 56, the Boston Symphony Orchestra, Inc.; pp. 57, 59, Hollywood Book and Poster; p. 58, U.S. Olympic Committee.

Front cover photograph, Gloria Kumagai. Back cover photographs: *upper left*, National Aeronautics and Space Administration; *lower left*, Walker Art Center; *right*, Patricia Saiki.

Interned Japanese Americans, California

THE *IN AMERICA* SERIES

AMERICAN IMMIGRATION
THE **AMERICAN INDIANS**, VOL. I
THE **AMERICAN INDIANS**, VOL. II
THE **ARMENIANS**
THE **BLACKS**
THE **CHINESE**
THE **CZECHS & SLOVAKS**
THE **DANES**
THE **DUTCH**
THE **EAST INDIANS & PAKISTANIS**
THE **ENGLISH**
THE **FILIPINOS**
THE **FINNS**
THE **FRENCH**
THE **GERMANS**
THE **GREEKS**
THE **HUNGARIANS**

THE **IRISH**
THE **ITALIANS**
THE **JAPANESE**
THE **JEWS**
THE **KOREANS**
THE **LEBANESE**
THE **MEXICANS**
THE **NORWEGIANS**
THE **POLES**
THE **PUERTO RICANS**
THE **RUSSIANS**
THE **SCOTS & SCOTCH-IRISH**
THE **SWEDES**
THE **UKRANIANS**
THE **VIETNAMESE**
THE **YUGOSLAVS**

Lerner Publications Company
241 First Avenue North • Minneapolis, Minnesota 55401